The Internet Marketing Dream

What life could and should be like for Internet Marketers

Alicia J. Beres

Copyright © Alicia J. Beres, 2022

All rights reserved. No part of this publication may be reproduced, distributed, or transmitted in any form or by any means, including photocopying, recording, or other electronic or mechanical methods, without the prior written permission of the publisher, except in the case of brief quotations embodied in critical reviews and certain other noncommercial uses permitted by copyright law.

The Internet Marketing Dream

Table Of Contents

Chapter 1
    Introduction - What Life Could and Should Be Like for Internet Marketers.
        The Internet Marketing Dream

Chapter 2
    Getting More Rest to Work More Productively
        The Value of Self-Control
        How to Improve Your Sleep with the Best Sleep Practices
        How to Always Get Out of Bed On Time
        A Sturdy Method for Waking Up

Chapter 3
    Developing Self-Control and Using Productivity Techniques
        Blocking Your Day: How to Do It
        How to Start Working Right Away

Chapter 4
    Hardware and Location
        A suitable computer
        Advice for a Successful Home Office
        Working While Moving
        How Internet Marketers Can Afford Better Technology
        What Internet Marketers Should Wear

Chapter 5
    Should You Become a Digital Nomad?
        Know Your Options, Nomads!

Chapter 6

The Internet Marketing Dream

Creating Work-Life Balance
    Create a Budget
    Keeping Work and Play Apart
    When You Need a Little Extra Money...

Chapter 7
    Finding and Managing Clients - How to Charge More and Work Less
        How to Get Rid of Difficult Customers and Simplify Your Life
        How to Do More Work While Working Less
        Having reasonable expectations
        Automation

Chapter 8
    Finding Meaning in Your Work

Conclusion

Chapter 1

Introduction - What Life Could and Should Be Like for Internet Marketers.

Congratulations if you're an online marketer that works full-time! You have joined a special club of self-starters with the passion, motivation, and technological know-how to create a career solely online and accomplish the lifestyle that millions of people across the globe have dreamt of.

Even if you aren't currently earning your full-time living from internet marketing, the fact that you have enough grasp of the idea to offer your services, advertise your website, or assist other people and companies makes you a real pioneer. The concept of producing money in this manner was entirely alien and unheard of only a few decades ago. We represent a new way of working and living in this undiscovered terrain.

But is it all you anticipated?

Are you using this special position that you have established for yourself?

Unfortunately, most of us will have to say "no" to this. Internet marketing can be very stressful, and if you don't put your health, lifestyle, and wellness first, it may even be worse than working a 9 to 5 job.

You may discover that you never really have a chance to unwind if you cannot distinguish between your professional and personal lives if you are preoccupied with worrying about whether you will have enough work, or if you feel entirely overwhelmed by a heavy job.

Similarly, if you don't establish a healthy pattern, you can work all day from home in your pajamas, beginning at 1 pm and concluding at 10 pm.

While waiting for this, some internet marketers may find themselves selling and performing things they don't like. Spending all of your time attempting to assist others in selling hazardous goods like steroids or low-quality digital goods may be a soul-destroying experience. Then there's the impression that your efforts are directed toward serving others and that you aren't really "progressing" in any significant sense.

The tax is another quite stressful factor.

Then there are the challenging customers who make excessive requests and complaints.

As you struggle to make ends meet, you could become worn out, unfit, anxious, and overworked. And once that happens, you could start to doubt if anything was worthwhile. You removed that

You took a bold step, dared to try something new, and became a digital marketer. And now your situation is worse than it was before...

The Internet Marketing Dream

If you know how to do it properly, an internet marketing lifestyle may look like this:

Internet marketing might first and foremost mean owning a successful firm of your own. Imagine having your own headed letter paper and being able to distribute cards with your branding on them. Imagine being successful enough to drive fancy automobiles and hire employees or freelancers. Of sure, having financial success is a wonderful feeling. But achieving financial success via perseverance and creativity is on a whole other level.

When someone asks you what you do for a job when you're at a party, it's simply a terrific feeling. You also get to say, "I own my own web company," to them. You'll feel like the ultimate boss since you'll have your digital kingdom.

You may experience the incredible independence of being self-employed while working online. I only just decided to skip work on Wednesdays. Why? I can, so I will! By doing it this way, I never have to work more than two days straight, and I get a day off while everyone else is at work. This enables me to run personal errands (banks and hair salons are empty) and take advantage of having time to play computer games or go for pleasant walks without fulfilling any social obligations. More significantly, it gives me the freedom to focus on my initiatives. Working "on" my company rather than "in" it, to maintain forward momentum and to continuously advance the enterprise.

You also have a variety of additional possibilities because of this flexibility. You may avoid this problem by ensuring you work out every morning before you start work if you are concerned about the health effects of a profession that, for example, entails nothing but sitting down all day.

Even better, you are now free to work anywhere you wish. Why not work remotely and become a digital nomad? Small cafés and pubs along the beaches let you operate while taking in the view of the globe. Alternatively, you can decide that you like your comforts too much and design a fantastic home office where you can work effectively.

You may discover methods to simplify your firm or make it run if you push this to the nth degree. By doing this, you'll be able to generate an entirely passive income, which means that you'll continue to make money whether you're dozing off or in the air traveling to your destination. Imagine having more money the next day.

Regarding This Book

It's time to modify your attitude to internet marketing and to begin selecting your lifestyle rather than allowing it to be pushed upon you.

All of those facets of the lifestyle of an internet marketer, in addition to many more, will be covered in this book. You'll discover how to create the lifestyle you desire by finding discipline and a rhythm in your job. You'll learn how to increase your output, enhance your health, increase your income, and seem and feel like the type of prosperous businessperson you undoubtedly imagined.

You will continuously learn how to expand your company and make it extraordinary so that you never feel like you are stagnant.

Chapter 2

Getting More Rest to Work More Productively

So, do you want to start earning more money as a digital entrepreneur? You want to learn how to increase your level of job satisfaction, income, and advancement.

It would help if you had a clear idea of your goals. However, it would help if you also modify your everyday workflow in smaller, more noticeable ways. You must be able to view the trees and the surrounding woodland. If you are a solo proprietor operating the business by yourself, you are both the CEO and the workforce, which puts you in an unusual and difficult scenario.

The issue is that you could get so bogged down by the routine tasks that you cannot see the logical course your company should follow. This implies that you are continuously struggling to remain afloat and cannot put in place the procedures that would give you the time to start working less or more effectively.

Because of this, many individuals who work online find themselves trapped in a loop of attempting to finish their job but not having enough time to take care of themselves or enjoy life.

Ironically, we must first pay attention to the minute details to allow ourselves enough time to concentrate on the broader picture. You are undoubtedly aware of your excessive workload and must fire your current clientele. You're certainly already aware of the possibility that there are better-paying customers out there who might enable you to make more money with less effort! But the odds are that you won't change anytime soon if you've been too hesitant to part ways with or bargain with your present clientele up until now.

We thus need a remedy to consider how you manage your existing workload. I'm ready to wager that you may be more productive and efficient. You are squandering hours of your day if you begin work at 1 pm or even 10 am. Similarly, you can be having issues with diversions or procrastination. Maybe calls keep coming in, and you can't seem to stop playing Doom for the first few hours every morning before you do anything productive.

Similar to this, there's a strong probability that the appropriate technology or simply a change in how you portray yourself might enable you to do a little more. And it will provide us the short-term breathing room we need to begin implementing change.

It's time to examine your working process and determine if you're organizing your days most effectively.

The Value of Self-Control

When you are in charge, it is very easy to let your lifestyle spiral out of control and to feel a little "all over the place" as you attempt to impose order and structure on your daily activities.

You're not being as productive as you might be if you begin your workday at 10 am and complete it at 10 pm. You must thoroughly reevaluate your strategy if you often complete work around 1 am. This will not only hinder you from spending time with your friends and family, but it will also give the impression to your customers that you lack professionalism. Do you want to collaborate with someone who consistently submits work just before the due date?

Additionally, you will become perpetually exhausted, frazzled, and less productive.

Starting to teach discipline is the answer, thus. That implies that you have a predetermined morning wake-up time and a defined start time for your workday. Likewise, it means that you are working at all times. This prohibits watching TV, playing video games, or making personal calls.

How to Improve Your Sleep with the Best Sleep Practices

Therefore, you're going to attempt to improve your sleep so that you have the willpower to quickly get out of bed and start working when the alarm goes off (or the gym). It takes a lot of mental discipline to do this, but that's part of the point—you'll develop discipline and become more successful and productive. If you can get out of bed at 7 am despite your body begging you to press the snooze button, you can accomplish anything!

But getting adequate sleep is the first step since it will give you more energy and willpower. Right now, this is highly "in-vogue," and several blogs and websites will go into great detail on "sleep hygiene."

You may take various actions to ensure your sleep is deeper, more restful, and more productive.

First, quit checking your phone and turn it off one hour before bed. The same is true for laptops, PCs, and other devices. To begin with, staring at bright displays will produce the stress hormone cortisol, which competes with the hormone melatonin that promotes sleep. Your body will create less melatonin the more cortisol is present. Phones and other electronic gadgets are also stressful in and of themselves. They are worrisome because we connect them to work, crucial calls, and angry consumers. However, they are also, biologically speaking, intrinsically stressful. This is because they include elements intended to arouse us and draw our attention. These include items like bright lights that flash, loud sounds, and red-letter writing that is bold.

Please turn it off, and your body will begin to unwind more. This is particularly true if you pair it with some reading, which can help you rest your thoughts and make your eyelids sleepy enough to make you feel ready for bed. People will likely believe you went to bed an hour earlier if you don't switch off your phone at this hour of the night.

Of course, if you're attempting to fall asleep, you need to make sure your bed is cozy and supportive and that the room is dark and silent. Consider purchasing blackout curtains, and cover or remove anything with an LED light at night.

The temperature should also be taken into consideration. Consider keeping a window slightly ajar to prevent nighttime tossing and turning since we tend to sleep more soundly and deeply when we are somewhat chilly. Your ability to sleep will also significantly improve after taking a warm shower. This promotes melatonin release while also assisting in muscular relaxation. Even better, it supports the body's ability to self-regulate temperature at night.

Additionally, you should consider your daily activities. Getting enough sunshine, exercise, and fresh air can help you sleep better and wake up feeling more rested.

Two Potent Supplements to Boost Your Energy, Sleep, and Learning

Still, having trouble falling asleep and staying asleep? Vitamin D is one effective dietary supplement you may utilize. When exposed to sunshine, our bodies naturally manufacture vitamin D, which has several important tasks, many of which revolve around the control and production of other hormones. When necessary, vitamin D may assist in increasing melatonin levels and can also increase testosterone levels, giving you greater energy. Unfortunately, most of us get too little sunshine, which leaves us severely vitamin D deficient.

Vitamin D may support the body's circadian rhythms since it is linked to sunshine.

The rhythms let us know whether we're hungry, exhausted, or otherwise. If you take this pill in the morning, you should experience better sleep and feel re-energized. According to more recent research, it is quite successful in preventing colds and the flu, maybe even more so than shots and pharmaceuticals. This is a significant plus since the flu, or a terrible cold may have a serious negative impact on your productivity for days.

Magnesium threonate is the other potent supplement I'm going to suggest. If you have trouble falling asleep, try taking this supplement before bed. You should notice that it helps you fall asleep quite fast.

Magnesium is a mineral that we get through our food and is essential for various bodily activities. In actuality, the body uses magnesium in over 300 separate chemical processes.

Magnesium may induce a somewhat tired, relaxed mood and is quite good in promoting sleep. Milk is often associated with rest because of magnesium. Additionally, it occurs.

Because of its capacity to extract calcium from muscle cells, be a potent muscle relaxant (which is involved in muscle contraction). In addition to all of this, magnesium is essential for the nighttime generation of testosterone.

For many individuals, magnesium works just as well as melatonin pills without the drawbacks or danger of reliance. Additionally, it offers several other health advantages, making it an excellent supplement.

Magnesium threonate is advantageous since the brain can

absorb it more easily. It has also been shown to improve "brain plasticity," a feature that helps to learn. This enables the brain to develop new neural connections and new neuronal growth!

How to Always Get Out of Bed On Time

The next step is to confirm that you are awakening when the alarm sounds. To wake up gradually is one of the most effective strategies I can provide in this respect.

NEVER press the snooze button. Although there is a strong temptation, doing so usually leaves you feeling more worn out than rejuvenated. The best option is to get out of bed gradually since you could discover that you lack the desire to do so. Why not get up and check your phone, for instance? Although it's common knowledge that we shouldn't check our phones first thing in the morning, if this is something you look forward to doing, it will be enough to make you sit up a little bit.

You could also discover that you can persuade yourself to sit up a bit and engage in conversation with your companion. or to switch on the TV.

This requires very little work, but you'll start to change if you do it. It will be simpler to get up in ten minutes than to go back to sleep!

A Sturdy Method for Waking Up

The appropriate tool will allow us to improve this once again. Here, we're referring to a "daylight alarm." This alarm comes with a strong light that mimics the sun's wavelength and progressively brightens up as dawn approaches.

It is intended that this lamp would mimic the morning sun as it rises, gradually becoming brighter and rousing you from slumber. The tools are designed to help those with SAD or seasonal affective disorder. However, they may be helpful for anybody who suffers with their energy levels in the morning for two reasons: first, they awaken you into a lighter sleep stage before the alarm goes off, making you feel less "jolted" when you wake up (a phenomenon known as "sleep inertia"). Additionally, when you wake up, the room seems light, which greatly increases your energy compared to waking up in a completely black space and fumbling for an unnatural-feeling bulb!

Chapter 3

Developing Self-Control and Using Productivity Techniques

You're standing now. What comes next?

You decide when you wake up and how long it takes to get ready. This will probably be related to other lifestyle obligations and demands. However, after you've decided to sit down and work, the next hurdle is to work without getting sidetracked or delaying it by procrastinating.

The main problem with procrastination is that it isn't enjoyable or relaxing. Most of us who procrastinate will mindlessly browse the internet, play phone games, or just generally waste time while feeling frustrated that we aren't working. Imagine how much more pleasant it would be to put in a full day's worth of work in the morning and then have a few hours at the end of the day to unwind and enjoy your independence!

So how can you motivate yourself to start immediately and keep working until everything is finished? You may do it by using the following advice.

Blocking Your Day: How to Do It

Make sure you do have upcoming times of leisure and enjoyment as the first crucial consideration. Your brain will likely oppose you if your goal when starting a job is to just work consistently from first thing in the morning to last thing at night. Unfortunately, most of us do not possess total control over our minds and emotions, and when we attempt to do so, we have difficulties.

If you know that you have 8 hours of serious work ahead with no break in sight, then that is when you are likely to struggle to remain concentrated.

Instead, you'll divide your day into manageable chunks that will include time for you to unwind and rest.

To achieve this, you must first consider what you need to get done that day and how much time you have left before signing out. Knowing how long it typically takes you to do any given work is another helpful nugget of knowledge.

This will then enable you to determine how long it will take you to accomplish each activity. Once you have that information, you may divide each work into time blocks of many hours and add breaks. Even if that "rest" is just for 10 or 20 minutes, it will be plenty to offer you something to strive towards and a break, both of which are crucial for your health above all else.

The following is an example of a day:

Monday

8 am to 9 am – Workout

9 am to 10 am - Work on Guest Posts for Client 1

10 am to 10:10 am – Prepare a cup of tea.

10.10 am to 11 am – Find new clients and reply to emails

11 am to 11.20 am - Mid-morning snack/magazine

11.20 am to 2 pm - Link Building for 3 Smaller Clients

2 pm to 2.30 pm - Lunch/episode of the favorite TV show

2:30 pm to 4 pm - Start design

4 pm to 4.10 pm: Make coffee

4.10 pm to 5.30 pm: Begin tomorrow's work

5.30 pm to 6.30 pm - Relaxation

You now have a day packed with several huge business initiatives, but it also offers you time to unwind, rest, and catch your breath. When you know that you can unwind with a cup of tea between 11 am, and 11.20 am, starting work isn't as unpleasant. And when you know you have a half-hour for lunch, working till 2 pm isn't that hard.

While many of us believe that the greatest way to be productive is to get right into work and avoid taking pauses, this is the worst thing you can do since your brain will 'resist' that and compel you to undertake more enjoyable or relaxing activities. Even if having breaks and snacks for hours may seem extravagant, you probably often take breaks for larger periods throughout the day. Only now you're using that downtime, recharging your batteries, and organizing and scheduling it.

Another thing that you may have noticed is that I've even scheduled when to consume tea and coffee. (Pro tip: a cup of coffee around 4 pm is a terrific method to perk yourself up after work when your body is most exhausted and sluggish.)

This is really quite crucial and will increase your productivity significantly. Why? As a result of the fact that little stops to make tea might really knock you out of the flow and constitute a greater gap in your productivity than you would anticipate. If you brew tea or coffee first, take a snack next, respond to emails after that... By the time 10.30 am rolls around, you may still have accomplished nothing! This is an extremely demoralizing emotion that might cause you to fall even further behind.

Instead, go to work straight soon on something necessary and significant so that you may start the day off well.

You'll have a significant "win" under your belt by 10.30 am, which will prepare you for the rest of the day.

Making sure that the time windows allotted for each task are greater than you anticipate they'll need to be is another suggestion for making this plan work. In other words, plan a task to take 2.30 hours if it generally takes you 2 hours to accomplish it. Why? You will feel confident in the system and capable of taking such breaks if you do so. When you're continually working under pressure, your work will suffer, you'll feel pressure to complete it, and you run the danger of not completing what you need to.

How to Start Working Right Away

What should be the first job you do each day is the following question. And the best way to do so is, in my opinion, to make the process enjoyable and reasonably simple.

Getting into the flow while working is easier said than done; the toughest part is getting into the right frame of mind in the first place. Once you get started, maintaining it is rather simple. The challenging part of traveling is getting to your destination in the first place.

If you choose a daunting, unpleasant, or extremely

boring task as your first one, you'll probably find yourself putting it off, coming up with justifications, and procrastinating. However, if you make it something amusing or somewhat simple, you can find that you get started with it far more quickly.

Nevertheless, make an effort to begin the day's work with the tasks that are more important and pressing. The idea is that if you approach burnout by 3 pm, you should have already finished all of the things that are the very most urgent. Once again, having this buffer will enable you to have greater faith in the system.

To "half complete" a job the day before is another helpful piece of advice in this respect. Start creating content, sending emails, constructing websites, or managing on-site SEO. We don't like unfinished business. Therefore this will make it much simpler to jump back in straight away the next day. That is to say because it is human nature to desire to finish a task that has already begun, you will find it much easier to get started.

Finally, forcing oneself to work is the greatest way to get over "writer's block," or whatever it is you're experiencing. Don't worry if your work is subpar or lacks inspiration; doing so may simply entail designing a few buttons or simply writing something down. Starting is the greatest approach to getting into the flow since you can always go back and edit your writing or creations.

Locate Your Way

For the next several days, try adhering to these suggestions and see how your workflow changes. You should discover that you are able to start reclaiming a portion of your day and so get some spare time. From there, we can begin examining ways to raise the standard of both your life and your company!

Chapter 4

Hardware and Location

Want to get more professional experience? Want to work more efficiently and more thoroughly?

Then upgrading the hardware you're using is an easy method to achieve that! You'll probably use this every day, in all probability. So why not ensure that it is enjoyable and that you are able to do as much work as you can?

A suitable computer

Create a fantastic home office as an excellent place to start.

Getting the correct computer that is capable of running all the applications you usually use is the first step in doing that.

In a later chapter of this book, I'll discuss the value of self-development—learning new talents to broaden your capacities. An illustration of this is learning 3D modeling. You can build gorgeous 3D logos, video openers, and more using 3D modeling. It may significantly broaden your skill set, help you stand out from other marketers, or assist you in strengthening your own identity.

You need power in order to carry out actions like this. Because of this, I suggest investing in a powerful computer with an i7 CPU that can be clocked up to 3 GHz and strong graphics capabilities. Your computer will become very future-proof and strong enough to run all the newest games with a GTX 1060, 1070, or 1080.

If you work in marketing, you'll probably write a lot, whether it's emails or blog posts. In any case, it's important to consider how this will impact the health of your fingers. You must take all necessary precautions to prevent the chance of RSI (repetitive strain injury), and one way to achieve this is to consider upgrading your keyboard.

Mechanical keyboards are the best keyboards for writers. These keyboards include keys that click satisfyingly. They are far more pleasant to type on and last longer than the membrane keyboards seen in budget laptops. The Cherry MX Blue switches are often regarded as the best switches for typing. I also like the rapid-fire keyboards since the actuation point may be reached with a bit less effort and strength.

To ensure that you like the typing experience, I advise testing out a couple of these keyboards in-person.

Finally, I advise purchasing an ultrawide monitor to finish off the experience. Because they allow for considerably more effective multitasking—allowing you to have many distinct things on the screen at once without constantly moving between tasks—ultrawide displays have been found to increase productivity by as much as 30%. Anyone who works with spreadsheets will find this to be great since you can extend them out wide and see several columns on a single screen at once.

Similar effects can be achieved with a multi-monitor setup, although it isn't ideal since the monitor bevels create a noticeable chasm in the center. A single monitor also takes up less space on your desk and requires fewer connections and cords than many monitors.

Advice for a Successful Home Office

Once your computer is set up, you can begin planning the rest of your office space around it. The area has to be welcoming and enjoyable for you to work in, which is a fundamentally important factor to take into account in this respect.

Making sure the office is in a separate area in the home is a smart place to start. It is crucial to do this because it will ensure that it doesn't easily become messy or disorganized (things that can prevent you from feeling relaxed while working). At the same time, you should make sure that your workplace is furnished with items that inspire you or that you just like being around.

For the most part, you will be working here every day. So why not make it a location you like being in? Do you feel inspired and motivated after hearing that? This is where some lighting and a few great decorations can really make a difference.

Maintaining order and cleanliness in the space is also important. Assure that your desk has a sizable surface area and that there are plenty of drawers available for storing a variety of products.

Working While Moving

As an online marketer, having a powerful computer and a base of operations may significantly improve your mental health. However, it's also a good idea to set up a "mobile command center." In other words, take the time to gather everything you'll need to be effective while working on the go, and make sure you like doing it.

Working at coffee shops can be an excellent option for you if you have trouble keeping focused and avoiding distractions, even with the suggestions we've provided in this book. Coffee shops provide a place to relax, free WiFi, and electricity. They also provide coffee, which is excellent for energizing the mind.

Nevertheless, due to their atmosphere, they are also very productive-friendly. You feel prepared to be productive because of the ambient noise of people chatting quietly, the aroma of the coffee, and the other people working on their various laptops.

Even better, you'll probably discover that working in coffee shops makes it difficult to become distracted. Because other people can see you, you won't feel like you should be watching YouTube or playing games. This is a great way to make yourself work hard and get into a productive frame of mind because you'll probably get to work with your head down. Every day of the week, I used to work at coffee shops, and although I would spend a significant bit of money on coffee, I discovered that I completed so much more work as a result.

Itself. Working in this manner allowed me to sometimes produce 30,000 words or more! I developed my productive attitude in this way, and as a result, I can now work from home almost as productively.

So what gear should you think about purchasing to build the ideal mobile command station?

Choosing a high-quality computer is important. This has to be an item that is finely built and enjoyable to use. Look for a comfortable keyboard and a display with a high resolution. Once more, you must be motivated to work on this and experience joy in doing so.

I heartily suggest Microsoft's Surface Pro series of products or its Surface Books. These computers run quickly, have good specifications and high resolutions, and are lightweight and portable. A lot more design work opportunities are opened up by the stylus's ability to write on the screen, and you can also sign off on Word and PDF documents.

Although little, things like this give your company a more professional appearance and boost your self-confidence as a worker. I started looking forward to working in cafes after switching from my old HP to a Surface Pro. However, I could now utilize Illustrator to create genuine vector graphics that could be used as logos. I was also able to start drawing ideas and learn how to code in Unity.

The equipment gave me a more polished feeling. It increased my self-confidence. It increased my capacity. And for all of those reasons, it enabled me to improve my career and increase my income. Spending is necessary for accumulation, and investing in superior technology can increase your income!

This is comparable to how investors operate. The reasoning behind this is that buying pricey products really increases a trader's likelihood of becoming a high-earning trader. It may sound strange, but you'll often find that by acting successful, you actually become one.

How Internet Marketers Can Afford Better Technology

But what if you can't afford this kind of improved technology? Even as a kind of investment? One solution is to take out a loan, and PayPal is an excellent method to accomplish so. You may apply for a loan via the "PayPal Working Capital" website if, like most online marketers, you now get your payments through PayPal. The excellent thing about this loan is that there is no deadline, and the interest is decided upon up front as a single price. However, it isn't the cheapest loan (a credit card loan is a better alternative, particularly one with 0% APR). Thus, you have the flexibility to pay it off gradually. Even better, payments are deducted immediately from your PayPal-delivered profits.

Therefore, if your daily income is $100 and you have to pay back your loan in 10% daily installments, you may increase your daily revenue by 10% until the debt is paid off without even noticing it. Even better, there won't be any fees or harm done to your credit score if you have trouble finding employment or your business is sluggish for any other reason.

Even better, you may deduct this from your taxes as an expenditure. This translates to a 30% discount on the price of new computers, new software, or anything else you use to improve your working environment and work process. And what's even better is that this also applies to the interest you pay, thereby reducing the cost of the loan by a third.

The good news is that most online marketers like technology; after all, it's probably why you started as a marketer in the first place. You can now buy all the fantastic stuff you've always wanted, such as a smart new phone, a terrific computer, a fancy keyboard, and a gorgeous monitor, without feeling the financial pinch thanks to these recommendations!

I'm ready to go one step further with this by constructing an "office pod" in our yard. Beautiful installation that will provide lots of light for a home office. It's built of glass, stands alone, and will offer me plenty of room for a big workstation and loads of technology. It's a no-brainer since it's tax-deductible, I can purchase it with PayPal working capital, and it will significantly increase the value of my house.

What Internet Marketers Should Wear

We've briefly discussed how to improve your technology

and how doing so might help you become a more effective digital marketer. However, I want you to consider updating your clothing as well.

This is crucial for in-person client meetings, particularly if you're a marketer who often seeks out customers in the real world. It's excellent for going to networking events as well. You know what else, though? Additionally, it's crucial for the "law of attraction" and your personal feeling of accomplishment. It's wise to dress for the job you desire rather than your one, as they say. You won't feel like working at your most productive level if you're presently unshaven and wearing a dirty t-shirt.

Consider the character in the movie Limitless who utilizes the brain-enhancing medication "NZT" to become an extremely successful trader, novelist, and ultimately politician. What does he do right away after taking the pill? His house is cleaned up, he has a haircut, and he dons a suit.

Similar to taking breaks, this seems indulgent, yet it is necessary for doing your best work. I suggest taking some time off the next weekend to revamp your outfit.

Chapter 5

Should You Become a Digital Nomad?

Working at coffee shops may boost your productivity, keep you from getting cabin fever, and put you in a setting where many others perform similar work.

But what if we went one step further with this? Why not pursue your ambition of working while traveling? Many of us want freedom and the opportunity to travel the globe, but you can as an internet marketer. Imagine enjoying breathtaking glaciers, mountain vistas, the northern lights, the Full Moon Party, and more while working on your laptop while relaxing in a café. That is the goal of being a digital nomad, and as an online marketer, you may easily achieve this goal. But does it fit you?

Know Your Options, Nomads!

Being a digital nomad seems to be the best option to "make the most of life." Since we only get one cycle to live in this world, there is a lot that most of us will never see. There is a vast world with many cultures, amazing views, experiences, and much more.

The Internet Marketing Dream

Other than when we're playing Skyrim (which is not the same!), most of us will never experience these things. Instead, we spend our days scribbling away at a computer and our nights watching TV. As we age, we lose out on having random discussions at beachside pubs.

With that in mind, it's difficult to see why someone would decide against being a digital nomad. This is a very wonderful experience for the appropriate kind of person.

But being a nomad also has drawbacks. One of the consequences of doing this is having to leave behind all of your creature comforts and relocate far from your loved ones. Being always on the go prevents you from taking a nice bath or binge-watching your favorite TV show. These

Even if they may not look great on Instagram, many of us still appreciate them, and for a good reason!

Being a digital nomad may not be for you if you have trouble with it and with not being able to see your closest buddy. Likewise, staying at home could be preferable if you want to expand your company as soon and effectively as possible. It will also be more difficult if you're in a relationship or a parent.

However, there are other options than becoming a digital nomad. This is but one example of "lifestyle design," and there are various methods to use the advantages of working from home and being self-employed.

For instance, even if you choose not to travel often, you can choose to do so a bit more often. Consider taking several mini-vacations all year long. Nowadays, you can fly for a very low price and stay in an Air BnB, making it inexpensive. Additionally, you can more easily finance the vacation since you can keep working while traveling. In this manner, you may still learn a lot and travel, but without feeling as if you have nowhere to call home.

Simply taking in more of your neighborhood is an additional choice. Coffee shops are one thing, but what about the library down the street, the beach if you live nearby, or an outdoor café? In your garden, perhaps?

I spent four years living in London, England, where I worked at large museums, on the docks sometimes, and occasionally with views of Big Ben. I was continuously looking for new workspaces to provide me with beautiful vistas while writing. Before that, when I lived in Bournemouth, I often sat on the beach and worked there as well as at the pubs close to the shore.

All of this was interspersed with frequent travels I took with my buddy, an internet marketer. One of my favorite work experiences was sipping beer and listening to wonderful music in a café in Zadar, Croatia (Schiller, it turned out). Warm and softly pouring, we could see people walking on the cobblestone streets below and the mountains in the distance. More recently, we conducted business in a Swiss mountainside chalet!

Chapter 6

Creating Work-Life Balance

No matter how much you like working in this environment or how productive and efficient you become, you will still need to think about how to strike a balance between work and pleasure. Many independent contractors struggle with this, and it's simple to see why.

The first and most important problem with this is that you may practically generate endless money when you work in industries like SEO, writing, or web design. Need extra money? work a couple more hours after that. It's that easy.

But by doing this, you have now put yourself in a position where you feel "guilty" whenever you unwind and allow yourself to get at ease.

Another issue is that because you operate online, clients may get in touch with you whenever they want. This problem is exacerbated if those individuals are located in other nations and work in various time zones. What can you do, then?

Create a Budget

You may have already picked up on the irony from reading the advice we've provided up to this point.

The easiest way to get more freedom and more free time is by putting more limitations on yourself. For instance, by setting up a more structured work plan, you may allow yourself extra time off and clock out sooner.

Similarly, oddly, setting up a budget for yourself might make you feel more liberated. The amount of money you need to survive should be determined after looking at all of your normal income and expenses. Likewise, consider

You should think about how much you'd want to save each month, how much you want to spend on treats, and how much cash you need to put up for taxes.

This is a crucial and helpful tip to keep in mind right away: as an internet marketer or anybody who is self-employed, paying taxes will be one of the biggest frustrations you experience. Get it out of the way by putting that money aside right away.

Having numerous accounts is a key piece of advice I should provide now. Divide your pay each time you get it into a billing, savings, tax, and allowance account. You won't be able to pay rent if you spend too much, and you'll also be able to avoid forgetting to set aside enough money for taxes at the end of the month.

Oh, and be sure to compute your taxes as soon as possible, so you have enough time to set aside the necessary sum.

You may choose how much money you need to make to live the lifestyle you desire, even if it may seem like a detour. This, in turn, implies that you know how many customers to take on and how much to charge, enabling you to select how late you can work.

By doing this, you are determining your own "pay" and, by extension, your own goals rather than putting yourself in a position where you feel pressured to work nonstop and make more money.

Keeping Work and Play Apart

As a result, you can specify how much work you must do before signing off. Ideally, you should also decide when you will cease working each day. Other obligations in your life may determine this or simply rely on how long it takes you to do the necessary tasks.

In any case, you may now define a day's worth of work and finish.

And now you have to be rigid about not returning emails, not accepting extra work, and not cramming more in. Remember that breaks will help you be more productive when you return to work.

A successful entrepreneur should have time to enjoy the fruits of their labor; otherwise, what's the point?

Having a separate work phone and separate business email is another way to keep work and pleasure apart. This will prevent you from being tempted to check messages when not at work.

It's crucial not to make any exceptions in this situation. Once you create an exception, you can bet that your customers will assume that you must always be on call to respond to messages or "just complete this piece of work." They won't intentionally take advantage of your spare time, but if they can, they will since that's just how people are. This must be a strict regulation, and if you find yourself working overtime, keep it a secret from them!

Another crucial aspect is to avoid reading emails. Even if you don't reply to an email, just being aware that it exists might cause tension and keep you from being able to relax and enjoy your job.

You'll use your free time on the weekends and evenings to focus on other elements of your life. You'll increase your strength at the gym during this time, and you'll also grow personally by traveling, making friends, and reading. You'll refresh your soul throughout this time.

And that's when you'll make friends and form connections. If you're an online marketer who finds it difficult to connect with people, think about whether you're giving yourself the chances you need.

Knowing that you're undoubtedly receiving crucial communications, you can't see may be stressful. Being upfront and truthful with your customers is the only way to resolve this. Inform them that you will only respond within certain hours. When you want to leave, let them know in advance. To ensure they get the message, set up an autoresponder if you're still worried.

When You Need a Little Extra Money...

One of the amazing things about being self-employed is the ability to make more money as and when you need it, to be able to buy everything you need by working a little bit longer.

If you are making yourself work a defined schedule, this may seem like a significant sacrifice, but you can still have your cake and eat it too. Once again, your limitations and your predetermined budget provide you with this alternative in this situation.

You are aware of your monthly expenses as well as your monthly income. Consequently, you have two choices whether you find yourself craving a new gadget or

The Internet Marketing Dream

longing to travel:

1. Save money in your "every day" budget until you have extra toward that endeavor.
2. To be able to buy that one item, you must work hard. When you have earned that much, quit!

You may have everything you want in this manner. Another fantastic perk of being an online marketer!

Chapter 7

Finding and Managing Clients - How to Charge More and Work Less

Instead of promoting your products, if you work as an internet marketer for clients, you'll have to deal with the customers, which is another challenging task.

Because, in many respects, working for a client is similar to working for a boss, there are similar obligations, need to follow directions, and time constraints. A customer does not, however, come with a contract, so they are free to quit giving you new work at any moment.

This puts you in a challenging scenario where you need all your customers if one decides to discontinue doing business with you. However, this also implies that you have to be accessible whenever they need you, which means there will be occasions when they give you too much work, and you wind up hurting your back trying to accomplish it all.

How precisely you respond to this is the question. The "tough" customer is a different problem. You may sometimes deal with customers with unreasonable expectations of you and discover that they often have issues with your job. Sometimes they'll just be obnoxious! This might add a lot of stress to your life.

Therefore you must once again find a solution.

How to Get Rid of Difficult Customers and Simplify Your Life

You should start by learning how to handle those challenging customers so that you may live a simpler life.

The ability to decline a job is crucial in this situation. It may be quite challenging to accomplish this, particularly if you have an anxious mind. But it's also crucial if you want to stop yourself from taking on unending quantities of work.

What kind of customers do you decline, then? One is the kind of customer who makes your life miserable. You would be better off dismissing such customers if you often have to adjust work that is completely good if you get harsh letters or have to cope with unrealistic demands. This is crucial since doing that job will eventually take more time and result in less accomplishment. Instead, concentrate on customers who make things easy for you so that you may do more and even provide more for them. Work for clientele who are deserving of your services.

This alters one's whole attitude as well. You are reminded that you are your boss when you are prepared to turn down the job. You collaborate because your goals are similar, and your talents and resources are complementary. Be prepared to say "no thanks" if a task is too huge or you don't like how it is done.

But always be courteous. No matter how nasty or ridiculous the customer is, responding is unprofessional and will ruin any chance of getting future business.

The second kind of customer is one who only ever places very few orders but requires an extensive conversation to get them. In my opinion, any customer who requests a Skype meeting is more likely to be someone who loves "playing" business than someone who would make a successful business partner. Reduce communication while increasing productivity. To achieve this, keep your customer list small and look for excellent clientele with positive working personalities.

How to Do More Work While Working Less

Another incentive to refrain from overloading yourself with work is that doing so will provide you the flexibility to take on new jobs that pay higher. You may post advertisements without desperation if paid a specific amount for your job and have a little more bandwidth to finish more. As a result, you may raise your price a little bit, and it won't be the end of the world if no one buys.

You may ask your current customers to submit bids for you if you have multiple clients paying a little bit extra. Inform them that your prices have changed and that you must now charge X dollars.

Although it is frightening to undertake, it is also quite logical and acceptable. Additionally, you'll be able to labor less or make more by raising your prices. Maybe both!

Even if you don't have any more work, try bargaining. If they refuse, the worst that can happen is that you simply keep doing what you're doing. Advice for internet marketers is to attempt giving extra for that increased amount if you're hesitant to do this. In other words, describe how your service is improved as a consequence rather than just asking for more money and ruining relationships.

Having reasonable expectations

Setting reasonable expectations is another piece of advice for online marketers who wish to avoid being overburdened with work. To put it another way, don't guarantee a customer that you'll bring them to the top of Google because you can't. Likewise, if you know you won't be able to create ten films for them each week, don't make that commitment.

One advantage of the company is that several bundles, including various services and goods, may be sold. You may easily alter the package to represent the kind of work that you excel at and like performing without having to write hundreds of thousands of words or create innumerable connections.

One final piece of advice is to attempt to locate a few customers that demand more work than you can provide them to keep yourself out of a situation where all of your clients have quit. Select a few willing to be flexible and take on more work as needed. Keep a record of your previous clients so that you may utilize it to entice new customers with discounts and other incentives. If the business is sluggish, contact your previous customers to inform them of your reduced packages.

Automation

What happens if you end up with too much work to handle? The best solution is frequently to automate or outsource. This could entail handing over your work to someone else and paying them slightly less than what you are paid to write it. Here is where you may begin assembling a team of independent contractors, giving you more time to concentrate on other projects or unwind and feel "being the boss."

Using tools and looking for methods to recycle outdated materials may help you do your task more quickly.

Chapter 8

Finding Meaning in Your Work

Now, you ought to have a lot better work-life balance and be earning more while making less money. Perhaps you're utilizing your newfound freedom to travel or unwind a little more.

However, you should also take a step back from your company and decide how and where you want to expand it.

If you are presently providing link-building services to clients daily, it's likely that you will eventually get weary and annoyed with your task. You don't know where you're going with it, and you're not doing the things you enjoy, so it's not gratifying.

Going more niche is one approach to resolving this. Instead of calling yourself an internet marketer, consider calling yourself a "fashion internet marketer" or a "fitness internet marketer." By doing this, you may help yourself stand out a little from the other marketers while also writing about the topics you like, interacting with websites you enjoy, and reading the topics you enjoy!

A further suggestion is to grow personally. We briefly

touched on this before, but when you begin to add new abilities to your repertoire, you'll be able to increase the scope of your services and advance professionally. This will allow you to charge more, wow your customers, and feel appreciated for what you do. Learning to write, design, and the program will broaden your horizons and provide you with new opportunities.

Analyze other revenue streams, explore how to expand your firm, and think about leveraging your marketing expertise to build your brand.

This might include developing a brand for your own company. When you have your company website, your company name, and a reputation that you are proud of, you will feel much more pride in what you do. Additionally, without you having to go out and find customers, this could help your business attract a lot more of them.

Consider also enlarging. Consider ways to expand your company, add more customers, and potentially outsource more of your job or hire inside workers.

Or maybe you might consider starting your blog? If you're writing about internet marketing, you may use this as a fantastic opportunity to demonstrate your abilities or to establish your credibility. But more than anything, starting a blog will give your company a new focus and offer you a sense of accomplishment. Working online has several benefits, including the chance to feel somewhat famous.

Conclusion

I hope you have some solid motivation and ideas at this point to start making changes to the way you manage your company. That entails altering how you deal with customers, ensuring that you don't spend hours putting off tasks every morning, and making your health and happiness your top objectives.

A career in internet marketing may provide you with a ton of independence, financial success, little recognition, and an unbelievable feeling of fulfillment. But to get there, you must work both in and in your company. The trip begins right here!

www.ingramcontent.com/pod-product-compliance
Lightning Source LLC
Chambersburg PA
CBHW050313220526
45465CB00005B/1966